Dear Elaine,
Crea

100 Magical Moments

Koerber

Create relationship magic, even if you are broke!

Tara Koerber

♥

Beatify Books
Kingmont, WV

Published by:
Beatify Books
PO Box # 140
Kingmont, WV 26578-0140
Beatifybooks.com

ISBN 0-9754760-7-6
Library of Congress Control Number: 2004093293

Dedications:

Mark
Blake
Caroline
I love you more than you could ever imagine.
All that I do, all that I am, is because of you.

And to my best friend, lover, and soulmate for believing in magical moments and making them with me.

Contents

Introduction

If your excuse for not being more romantic has simply been that romance is too expensive, then this book can recharge your relationship. There are 100 ideas detailed to create romance and passion in your life, even if you are broke. You cannot afford to NOT be romantic! Love without cultivation will stagnate. Boredom can sneak in and one may wonder where all the fireworks have gone. Hopefully, with the use of this book you can begin to see romance in a new light. Use these ideas to transform your ordinary moments into magical ones. I challenge you to make romance a priority in your life. There is no need to settle for mediocrity. With just a little effort, you too can create some magic! Abracadabra.

"A successful marriage is an edifice that must be rebuilt every day."

-Andre Maurois

♥ ♥

♥

♥

1. Pillowcase Notes

Take an old pillowcase and surprise your mate with a unique message. Using fabric paint write words such as, "Make me late for work." Other suggestions could include, "Wanna relive my dream?" and "Dreaming of you…" Place the pillow on his side of the bed.

♥

2. Treasure Hunt

Leave little clues around the house that eventually lead to a very small gift. Mine culminated in a trip to the mailbox and a 25 cent piece of beef jerky and a lotto ticket. You don't have to have money to show that someone special how much you care!

♥

3. The Sweetest Key ring

Transform your sweetheart's key ring into something special. Attach a cardboard key with the following inscription, "Key to _____ 's heart."

♥

4. The Creative Bouquet

Instead of flowers bring home a bouquet of cards. Let your partner know how special he/she is. Include some of the reasons you fell in love in the first place. You may also bring home a bouquet of lollipops or another favorite candy!

♥

"Love is composed of a single

soul inhabiting two bodies."

-Aristotle

♥

♥

5. Cupid Tracks

Have your lover follow the footprints of Cupid to find her present on Valentine's Day. For an added touch, use red construction paper to make a bow and arrow to leave at the gift site.

♥

6. Favorite Tunes

Set your baby's favorite radio station in the car. You can also leave a favorite CD. If you feel ambitious, use your computer to create a CD composed entirely of his/her favorite tunes. Entitle it, "___ 's Greatest Hits!"

"Love is a little haven of refuge
from the world."

-Bertrand A. Russell

♥

7. Signs

This is one of my favorite things to do to show my partner how special I think he is. Leave huge signs all over the house letting your mate know just how much you appreciate him. You can use markers, crayons, or even print them on the computer. A huge RED font will be sure to grab his attention. Hang the signs all over with scotch tape, including going down the staircase, by the toilet, even under the shades. I used phrases like: "I love how well you take care of me." You are sexy!" and "You make me happy!"

♥

8. Childhood Libations

Make your lover's favorite childhood drink and bring it to him/her. Examples include: a chocolate malt, a Shirley temple, or an egg cream. To make a Shirley temple use a beverage such as 7-up and add a little grenadine to it. Top it off with a cherry and an umbrella and your mate will be touched you remembered!

♥

9. Stroking

Brush her hair 100 strokes every evening.

♥

10. Mix and Match Holidays

On Halloween dress up as Santa and deliver candy canes shouting, "HO-HO-HO, Happy Halloween!"

♥

11. Tie Clip

Have his tie clip engraved with a meaningful phrase for the both of you. The phrase I had engraved read, "I Choose Us".

♥

12. Lights

Using Christmas lights, make the shape of a heart. Place it in your bedroom or in one of the windows. Have it lit in the evening so your partner sees it aglow!

"I love you, not for what you are,
but for what I am when I am with
you."

-Roy Croft

♥

13. Picnic

Have a surprise picnic in the car on a rainy day! You can cut out cheese in heart shapes for cheese and crackers. Bring a candle and soft music. What may have been a gloomy day will be transformed to blissful!

♥

14. Joke of the day

Start the day off with a giggle. Take turns being the "bearer of the joke." You can leave a written joke under the pillow, inside the refrigerator, with her coffee, on the steering wheel of the car, etc. You can write silly jokes or cut out a comic. What a sweet tradition!

♥

15.Exploding Kisses

Want to create some fireworks of your own? Buy some Pop Rocks and keep them in your mouth the next time you kiss your love!

♥

16. Bedroom Forest

For those with some artistic ability, paint a tree on your bedroom wall. Place your initials on the trunk of the tree.

♥

17. Birthday Wishbook

This gift is extremely special because it shows you pay attention. Create a small booklet decorated with your own artwork of all of your mate's fanciful wishes. Include things you cannot afford and even make things up. The point is to show your lover all the things you'd like to give if only you could afford to. Perhaps you'd like to give her the world, then include an illustration of the earth! Some humorous examples I have included in my wishbook are: a house elf to wash the dishes, a self-propelled lawn mower, fancy cars, trips to Paris, and expensive jewelry are other fanciful examples.

♥

♥

18. Wishing Well

Build a surprise wishing well for your mate made out of legos. You can also use boxes or even draw a picture. Attach a small note stating, "May all your wishes come true." Remember to include a penny!

♥

19. Floating Candles

Instead of floating candles in a bathtub, try placing them in an unexpected place like the kitchen sink.

♥

"Love is, above all, the gift of oneself."

-Jean Anouilh

♥

♥

20. Strike a Pose

Buy a small stuffed animal for your sweetheart to place on your bed. Position it differently every day. Use it to deliver love letters.

♥

21. Take me to Heaven

Let your dearest walk into a room full of clouds. Purchase several bags of cotton candy from the grocery store. Hang them from the ceiling. Tell your mate how thankful you are because having him in your life is like being in heaven. To really make an impression, draw a picture of a gate and hang it on the door. Put a sign across the top that reads: The Pearly Gates.

♥

22. Puppy Love

Go to the local animal shelter and adopt a pet. Present your love with this symbol of your affection and then name it after her.

♥

23. Sweet Awakenings

Awaken your spouse to the music of "your song."

♥

"Love is friendship set on fire."

-Jeremy Taylor

♥

♥

24. The Bank of Love

Show your appreciation for all of the things your partner does. Present your sweetie with a weekly or monthly statement from "The Bank of Love." Design it to look like a statement you receive from your checking account. Deposits can include things like: taking out the trash, bathing the kids, and rubbing my neck. Use dollar amounts to show how much you appreciate certain items. Running a bubble bath could be worth ten thousand dollars. Total the account and declare yourself rich in love!

♥

♥

♥

25. You Fit me to a T

Use one of your old worn out t-shirts to write a love letter on. Perhaps you'd prefer to keep it simple and write in large letters, "Perishable- Unwrap Tonight!" You can even use washable markers. Wear the shirt around the house and wait for your spouse to read it.

♥

26. Lollipop Dreams

Propose to your partner for the first or second time using a lollipop diamond ring. Your partner will never tire of hearing all the reasons you can't live without him.

♥
27. Book of Love

Write her a novella. Make her your heroine and tell a story of your passionate love affair.

♥
28. Warm Drive

Brush the snow off of her car in the morning and warm it up. Be sure to place a hot cup of cocoa or coffee in the drink holder.

"Love is a canvas furnished by nature and embroidered by imagination."

-Voltaire

♥

♥

♥

29. Yard Card

Make a huge lawn card and place it in your front yard. Make a giant heart for Valentine's Day, or a birthday teddy bear, an anniversary champagne glass, or a stork for a new baby.

♥

30. Give her the Moon

Wait until evening falls and secretly set up a place outside with warm blankets and pillows. Cover her eyes and bring her outside. Surprise her with a secret viewing of the moon and the stars. Sip champagne, tea, or hot cocoa. Remember to make a wish!

♥

31. "Give this to Mommy, Please..."

If you have children use them as a secret messenger. Tell your child to whisper into mommy's ear, "Daddy says, he loves you." Variations could include how pretty mommy looks. This is especially charming when done out in a public place like a restaurant or a crowded store.

♥

"You will find as you look back upon your life that the moments when you have truly lived are the moments when you have done things in the spirit of love."

-Henry Drummond

♥

♥

32. La Restaurante

Create your own menu for your spouse. Invite him to dine at La Tara. Include childhood favorites on the menu. Desserts could include kisses a la mode, or hugs. Make sure to wait on your mate hand and foot.

♥

33. High School Notes

Have one of your children deliver a love letter folded like a note from high school.

♥

34. E-mail an "I Love You"

If you have a digital camera, take a photo of yourself holding a sign that says, "I love you." The sign can say anything from I miss you, I need you, or can't wait until you get home baby!

♥

35. The Campfire

Guys hunt and gather. Build her a roaring campfire. (Make sure it is legal to do this where you live before doing this one.) Roast hot dogs and marshmallows. Sit around the fire and tell stories. Tell her the story of how you first fell in love with her.

"The love we give away is the only love we keep."

-Elbert Hubbard

♥

♥

♥

36. Lord of the Rings

In order to get his birthday present this year, your sweetie has to find "the ring." You can buy it for a quarter at the grocery store and leave it inside its bubble. Hide it and give your partner clues to find it. When the ring is retrieved, you will give your partner his real present! Here is a sample letter engaging the birthday love in his hunt:

Dearest Lord of the Rings,
You are the decider of the fate of Middle Earth. Maximize your powers if you wish to find your birthday present. The only way to receive your present is to obtain the precious ring and present it to an elfin beauty. It is only then that she will present your gift to you. Beware of Dark Riders.
Good Luck My Lord!

♥

37. Magic Dust

Grab a small box. Decorate it as creatively as you dare. Place a small note inside stating, "Here is some magic dust. It is guaranteed to cheer you up. Use it whenever you want to feel happy!" You can place glitter inside or just leave the box empty. The important part is that your lover will see how important his/her happiness is to you.

♥ ♥ ♥ ♥

♥

38. Dinner by the Fire

On a rainy day, prepare a romantic dinner to be eaten by the fireplace. Here is the kicker: You do not need to have a real fireplace! Do what I did. Take several pieces of plain white paper and tape them together. Draw a roaring fire, or something that closely resembles one, and tape it to the wall. Send an e-mail or make a phone call saying, "Gosh wouldn't it be nice if we could curl up by a fireplace tonight?" Make sure to surround it with candles so it looks real and serve dinner when your love comes home!

♥

"Love doesn't make the world go 'round; love is what makes the ride worthwhile."

-Franklin P. Jones

♥

♥

39. Oil his Car

Tape a bottle of massage oil to the windshield of his car. Make your own personalized label for the oil and tape it on. Mine looked like this:

> *Patient: Lover's name*
> *Medication: Libido Enhancing Massage Oil*
> *Dosage: Several seductive strokes*
> *Refills: See prescribing physician*
> *Physician: Doctor of Love, (pet name here)*

As an added touch, send an e-mail saying you have noticed signs of withdrawal: missing wife, agony from being apart and recurrent thoughts of wife. Diagnose him with "---itis." Insert your name and add the suffix "itis." Prescribe a heaping dose of love from you! Can you imagine his anticipation to get home once he finds the massage oil!

♥

40. Grinning Babies

Use a digital camera to take a picture of your child(ren). Make sure to choose a photo with an absolutely huge grin. E-mail the picture to your mate at home or work. I know I was elated when I received an e-mail like this. I cannot express how much it brightened my day!

♥

41. Hide n Seek

Choose some of your favorite quotes and make it a fun ritual of hiding "the quote of the day" in your mate's pockets, vitamin bottle, coffee mug, alarm clock, or even taped to the steering wheel of the car!

My personal favorite quote written to me by my lover:

I fly between the stars when you smile – J.K.

♥

♥

♥

"A coward is incapable of exhibiting love; it is the prerogative of the brave."

-Mahatma Gandhi

♥

42. Grapes

I will never forget when jokingly I told my lover to fan me and feed me grapes. The next day he emerged from the kitchen with a bowl full of grapes. I couldn't believe that he had paid such close attention to what I had said. I felt amazed by this act of servitude and relished the attention!

♥

43. Wrap u up in my Love

Print out pictures of you and your mate on the computer. Tape them together and wrap a present in it. It works really well with CD's and DVD's. Give her a copy of the first movie you ever saw together!

♥

"There is no remedy for love but to love more."

-Henry David Thoreau

♥

♥

44. Sidewalk Charm

I once drew a blazing hot sun, with my limited artistic abilities, and wrote in huge letters, "You are HOT!" Yes, he smiled from ear to ear. On another occasion, I adorned the sidewalk with colorful flowers leading up to the door and wrote, "I missed you!" The messages eventually washed away in the rain but left a lasting impression. If you feel bold, make a public declaration with an "I love you," "Happy Anniversary," or "Happy Birthday," as large as you can possibly write. Do this in the middle of the street for all to see!

Find a quotation, and use it to make your point.

♥

45. Interesting Location

Try to leave love notes in neat places. The coolest place I have found a love note was in my makeup compact. I had gone out of town and was really missing my mate. I went about my normal routine of applying my makeup when I found a yellow sticky note attached to the mirror. It read:

My Dearest Love,

Miles may separate us, but my heart, soul, and thoughts are with you.

All my being,

J.K.

♥♥♥♥♥♥♥

"To love someone is to see a miracle invisible to others."

-Francois Mauriac

♥

♥

46. Wanna Play?

Do this idea when you are feeling adventurous. Using a digital camera take some risqué photos of yourself. Attach a note to your bedroom door that reads, "Wanna play?" Then inside, on the bed, have the digital camera sitting with another note stating, "Wanna see?" Imagine the surprise when your mate finds the photos. (Remember to erase the photos later!)

♥

♥

47. Father's Day Olympics

Hold an annual Father's Day Olympic Games. This idea is very exciting for all those involved. It is a blast to plan with the other moms and the dads are eager participants. It can become a very fun tradition. I change the theme annually so the guys never know what to expect on their day. The guys compete in silly games and are even awarded prizes. (See the quick start guide at the back of the book for some sample events and invitation letters.)

♥

♥

48. Priceless Tulips

I once received the most delicious breakfast in bed with flowers. They were tulips. These beautiful flowers are symbolic of great love. In fact, in ancient Turkey they could only be grown for royalty. Possession of this flower by someone in a lower class was against the law and punishable by exile. My flowers were not very fragrant, but nonetheless special. You see they had been printed out on the computer from a flower website. They did not cost a penny but they were priceless.

♥

"Love does not consist in gazing at each other but in looking outward together in the same direction."

-Antoine De Saint-Exupery

♥

♥

49. The Refrigerator Hanging

I used quotes from e-mails and cards of nice things others had written about my sweetheart. I wanted him to be reminded of how wonderful everyone thought he was. I included quotes from his instructors such as, "Your performance is first class." Then I hung it on our refrigerator so he would know how proud I am of him.

♥

♥

50. Wash and Wax

Wash and wax your mate's car. Make sure you even fill the car up with gas. Return the sparkling car complete with a note attached to the steering wheel that reads, "Start me up baby!"

♥

51. Bake a Cake

Once my partner had gotten a really good grade in a class he had struggled with. I baked him a delicious chocolate cake and wrote a very special message with icing. It said, "You are brilliant!" Tell your partner that he is sexy, special, or wonderful. A sweet message and it's edible too!

♥

52. Birthday Bonanza

On your baby's birthday give her as many presents as she is years old! If she is turning thirty-three write down thirty-three reasons you love her and place them inside thirty-three balloons. Give her thirty-three M&M's, thirty-three kisses, thirty-three "I Love You's," and thirty- three candles on the cake you and the children bake. (All of this for under $20.00.) Did I mention romance doesn't have to be expensive?

♥

"We don't remember the days; we remember the moments."

-Cesare Pavese

♥

53. Pamper Your Princess

Paint her toenails. Give her a massage. Tell her how lucky you are.

♥

54. Tea Please

Bring her a surprise cup of tea when you are both working in separate ends of the house. Kiss her cheek softly and go back to what you were doing. The night will be so much sweeter.

♥

55. The Greatest Fan Evening

Write your love a letter stating all the reasons you are her biggest fan. Accompany the letter with a pretty oriental fan or if you cannot afford to buy one, fold a simple fan out of paper to present as a gift. Finally, play her the love song, "I'll Be," by Edwin McCain.

♥

56. Birthday Flowers

Pick her fresh flowers on the birthdays of all your children. Thank her for giving you such beautiful children.

"For love is heaven, and heaven is love."

-Sir Walter Scott

57. Sexy Screensaver

Surprise your mate by leaving a sexy screensaver on the computer. Using your digital camera take some sexy photos of yourself for your lover to enjoy. If you do not have a digital camera but you have a scanner, use it to scan a tempting picture. Include some enticing words as well.

♥

♥ ♥ ♥

♥

58. The Report Card

Hang a relationship report card on the refrigerator for your mate to find when he gets up in the morning. Be sure to give him an A+ in lovemaking. Under the comments section be sure to thank him for last night and declare him a sex god!

"Love is a taste of paradise."

-Sholom Aleichem

♥

59. Surprise Message

At a time you are expecting a phone call from your sweetheart, change the outgoing message to, "Sorry I cannot come to the phone right now. I am busy being madly in love!"

♥

60. Cookies and Milk

Bake him a homemade batch of warm, gooey chocolate chip cookies. Serve a glass of ice cold milk with them and watch him melt!

♥

61. "Can I Have This Dance?"

This idea is inspired by my father in law, Don. He and his bride, Linda are still happily married after all these years because he knows how to make her feel loved through the small details of an average day. He also knows how to sweep her off her feet when he wants to. One evening he met her at the door and invited her to dance with him. He already had the song, "May I have this dance for the rest of my life," by Ann Murray, playing in the background. They danced together and then he whisked her out onto the patio and served her dinner, which he had prepared *himself*.

♥

62. Rub his Feet

When he has had a hard day at work, welcome him home with a good foot massage. Use some soothing cream with a relaxing scent like lavender. Watch as the stress dissipates from his body. Rub his neck, too!

♥

63. "Honey" I love you.

Leave a trail throughout the house with small packets of honey. At the end of the trail, leave a note stating, "It must "bee" love!" Use your imagination and have lots of fun licking the honey off of one another's bodies.

♥

64. Spic and Span

Surprise her one day when she goes to the grocery store or off to work. Have the house sparkling and dinner already started. She will be incredibly grateful!

♥

65. The Red Hot Evening

Leave the song, "I'm on Fire" by Bruce Springsteen in the cassette player of his car. Attach a note that says, "Play me." When he walks in the front door have him find a message written in red lipstick that says, "I'm hot for you tonight." Leave a trail of candy red hots that lead to you in the bedroom waiting in red lingerie.

♥

66. The Driver

Have a close friend dress up in a suit and tie and pretend to be your driver for the evening. Have him take you to a lovely park where you can pop open the trunk equipped with candles and blankets and have a surprise picnic.

♥

♥

♥

67. The Honey Do List

Transform the traditional To Do List into an endearing gesture. Entitle it the Honey Do List. Be sure it doesn't contain any practical items. Items could include: receive a passionate kiss, get a neck massage, receive a loving gaze, receive sexual favors etc.

♥

♥

"Love is the greatest educational institution on earth."

-Channing Pollock

♥

68. The Most Relaxing Bubble Bath

In the midst of utter chaos when the kids are cranky and you could cut her stress with a knife it is the opportune time to perform this act of servitude. Run her a bubble bath and take the kids to play at the park. Let Calgon take her away as she enjoys some peace and quiet.

♥

♥

69. Favorite Color Day

Celebrate her favorite color throughout an entire day. For example, if her favorite color is pink serve her some strawberry milk with pink flowers. Send her love notes written on pink paper. Wear a pink shirt and cook pink pancakes for dinner!

♥

♥

70. Window Box

Place a window box outside her window with fresh flowers. If you cannot afford to buy them then sprinkle some seeds and let her be surprised when they bud!

♥

71. Muse Resume

Apply for the position of his muse. Present him with a resume that includes all your sexy skills and perhaps attach a seductive photo. I'm sure he will enjoy the interview to see if you get the position!

"Our heart has reasons that reason cannot know."

-Blaise Pascal

♥

♥

72. The Locket

Give her a heart shaped locket. Insert a tiny photo of you and your children. It will probably become her most treasured possession.

♥

73. Perfume

If you cannot afford to buy her some of her favorite perfume, ask for some samples at the department store. Write her a letter explaining why she epitomizes the perfume you are giving her. If you give her Beautiful list all the reasons that she is the most beautiful woman in the world to you.

♥

74. Sweet Dreams

Spritz her pillow with the soft scent of
lavender and place a love letter
underneath for her to find when she
climbs into bed. She will definitely
have sweet dreams!

♥

75. Lusty Libations

Create your own custom label for a
bottle of your love's favorite drink. It
can be placed on anything from a
plastic bottle of coke to a fine bottle of
wine. Call the drink Lusty Libation.
List the ingredients as passion, desire,
and love. Include a warning that states
imbibing this love potion could result
in intense passionate lovemaking!

♥

76. Erotic Fortunes

Send him erotic fortune cookies at work. You can order these from Red Envelope. You can request a catalog, order by phone, or online at www.redenvelope.com.

♥

77. Be his Calendar Girl

For around twenty dollars you can create a custom calendar. Use seductive pictures if you want and hang the new calendar in his garage!

♥

"Passionate love is a quenchless thirst."

–Kahlil Gibran

♥

♥

78. The Photo Watch

Order a watch for him that shows off pictures of your children from www.Personalcreations.com.

♥

79. Fireworks

A lot of men love to set off fireworks. If it is legal to set them off where you live, buy a small box to set off together. End the evening by making some fireworks of your own!

"The best and most beautiful things in the world cannot be seen or even touched. They must be felt with the heart."

-Helen Keller

♥

80. Daisy Petals

Use the petals of some daisies to spell out a love message for your dearest.

♥

81. Hand Massage

Traveling together can get a little stressful particularly with airport delays and layovers. Pack a small bottle of lotion to give him a surprise hand massage with. It is not only incredibly thoughtful but also is a huge tension reliever.

♥

82. You Melt Me

Make him an ice cream sundae with hot fudge on top. Surprise him with it along with a note that reads, "You melt me."

♥

83. You Light Up My Life

On a lovely evening go outside and catch a firefly. Place it inside a jar with holes in the lid. Present it to your love with a note that says, "You light up my life." Later that evening set the firefly free together.

♥

84. Burning Love

Attach a heart shaped note to the outside of the oven that reads, "Your love warms my heart."

♥

85. Serenade

Shut off her alarm before it goes off in the morning. Open her window and gently awaken her. Tell her the birds are singing to her.

♥

"People who are sensible about love are incapable of it."

-Douglas Yates

♥

♥

86. Silly Prunes

The gift is a box of prunes. The note states, "I love growing old with you." Sound a little corny? Perhaps, but love involves taking risks. At least you tried to express love. Romance is love set to motion.

♥

87. Runaway Love

Attach a note in the shape of a heart to her running shoes. Write the words, "You have run away with my heart." Rent the movie Runaway Bride and watch it together.

♥

88. The Globe

Give him a globe. Attach a note that says, "You mean the world to me."

♥

89. Love in a Bottle

Float a bottle in her next bubble bath. Be sure to place a sweet love letter inside the bottle!

♥

90. Block Tower

Using your children's blocks assemble a tower that reads, "I love you."

♥

91. Say it with Food

Using a knife, etch the words, "I love you," onto cream cheese, peanut butter, the stick of butter, or a block of cheese.

♥

92. Shower him with Love

Attach a note to the shower handle that says, "I want to shower you with love." Wash his hair and his back for him. Dry him off with a towel that has been warmed in the dryer.

"Let us not love with words or tongue but with actions and in truth."

-1 John 3:18

♥

♥

♥

♥

93. Twizzler Surprise

Using your lover's favorite candy, spell out a love message. I used Twizzlers. They make fantastic letters.

♥

94. Mother's Day Handprints

On Mother's Day, give her a potted plant from your children. Transform an ordinary pot into a treasure by placing your children's hands in paint and putting their handprints on the sides of the pot. Print the word, " MOM," on it and it has become a magnificent work of art!

♥

95. The Care Package

When your sweetheart is sick be sure to bring home a care package. It can include favorite magazines, movies, tea, popcorn, tissues with lotion, medicine, a teddy bear, and a balloon.

♥

96. Angel

Show her that she is your angel by giving her a pair of wings. Make them out of construction paper or whatever you wish. Have her open the present and tell her that she is your angel and that she makes you fly.

♥

97. Doughnuts

Surprise her by bringing her a box of doughnuts at work to share with her coworkers.

♥

98. Pot of Gold

Draw a picture of a rainbow and place a photo of her at the end of it. Attach a note that says she is your pot of gold.

♥

"Love is an irresistible desire to be irresistibly desired."

-Robert Frost

♥

♥

99. Acts of Servitude

Sensuously shave his beard for him.

♥

100. Surprise Scrapbook

Make a scrapbook with photos you've taken and surprise her with it. Include special moments you have shared and things you want to remember.

♥

♥

And finally, the most important magical moment of all: Gratitude

Everyday thank him for at least four things. Even small things are important. Tell him you are grateful that he took out the trash, bathed the kids, and changed the oil in the car. A person who feels appreciated feels loved. Never take your partner for granted. Focus on the positive. Finally, never never become complacent.

♥ ♥

The Insightful Question:

If you were on a deserted island with your lover, how would you romance him/her?

Compose a list of 10 things you would do on that island and compare your list with your partners. Did you focus on basic needs such as food and shelter or did you try and bring the things your partner is most passionate about alive on the island? Do you make your partner sparkle?

Here is a sample of my own Top Ten List:

1. I'd write I love you in the sand with a stick.
2. I'd climb to the top of a tree to find the perfect coconut- no bananas for my baby! (He hates bananas!)
3. I'd lay and count the stars with you.
4. Somewhere, somehow I'd find dead cow on that island and cook it on a fire! (He loves steak!)
5. I'd pick you wild flowers.
6. I wouldn't sing to you. (I sing horribly!)

7. I'd do a seductive striptease around our campfire.
8. I'd give you a hot stone massage with rocks I had found.
9. I'd bring you a pet monkey.
10. Do you prefer me to remain naked or wear a sexy display of seashells and leaves?

-I'd rub your feet.

Conclusion

Unfortunately, as much as we hate to admit it, relationships take work. Creating a thriving relationship means choosing a life of eternal courtship. There are all kinds of stressors in life that pull us away from giving our relationship the energy it deserves. The demands of work, children, finances, household chores, can drain the sparkle from our love life. We believe that this love we have will remain and that comfortable is something worth settling for.

If you want a great relationship you have to work at it each and every day. The infamous analogy of a relationship and a flower garden perfectly illustrate this point. If you want flowers instead of a patch of weeds you must water your garden every day. Whether you say it, write it, make it, or buy it, put your love to action. It takes one minute to write, "I love you," on the bathroom mirror with a bar of soap. Be brave enough to infuse a little magic into your wilting relationship or make a great one even more radiant! When you place your head on your pillow each night be able to answer the question, "What have I done today to show my love how very much I care?" If you don't have an answer, get up and do something.

The Quick Start Guide

Sometimes we all need a little help getting things started. This section will make it easy to recapture, or create, your romantic self. Follow the ideas to get started. As you begin to feel comfortable with being romantic, feel free to get imaginative. Add activities or change ideas to fit your relationship. This guide is not set in stone, change it around, and make it work for you. Create your own magical moments!

It takes most of us at least a month to create a good habit and even longer to break a bad one. Use this for the first month, and then, make it a priority to continue.

Week One:

Monday: When you can find a few minutes of alone time, write down two quotes. This is idea number 41. You can even use some of the ones from this book! Check the index for a listing of included quotes.

Tuesday: Place one of the quotes someplace it will definitely be found. Do not hide this one. Leave it on the refrigerator door, on the coffee maker, or bathroom mirror.

Friday: Hide the second quote someplace different. Do not use the same spot as Tuesday! Feel free to show a little imagination, but make sure it will be discovered.

Week Two:

Monday: Use idea number 45. Write a love letter and hide it someplace it will be found. Include the reasons why you fell in love in the beginning. Then, let your mate know why you love him or her even more now!

Wednesday: It is time to hide a quote! Do it just like you did during week one.

Weekend: Pick a nice evening when you can settle down and relax together. Use idea number 30 to give your love the moon! If this does not fit into your busy weekend schedule, rearrange things. Do this during the week and hide a quote over the weekend.

Week Three:

Monday: Hide your quote. If it seems like you are doing this a lot, you are! Hopefully, you are enjoying leaving the quotes and your mate is enjoying finding them. Remember, you can always change to a different idea that fits your relationship better.

Tuesday: Find a few minutes of alone time. Use the time to prepare idea number 3. Make your mate a key ring!

Wednesday: As schedules permit, put the key you made yesterday on your love's keys. Try to do it in the morning so your mate can enjoy the feeling all day! If you have to, put it on the key ring Tuesday night.

Friday: Hide a quote! This might be a good day to leave a joke as well. If you leave both, put the joke where it will be found first. Then the romantic quote will be found second, leaving your love a warm feeling all day!

Weekend: As schedules permit, plan for idea number 44. You may have to buy the sidewalk chalk sometime during the week, if you do not have any around the house. It is really inexpensive. Your loose change should be enough. When your love is out for a few minutes, or sleeping, decorate the driveway or sidewalk!

Week Four:

Monday: Find some time to find two quotes to use later in the week. This is also a good day to prepare magic dust. It is idea number 37. You will be using it tomorrow.

Tuesday: It is time for magic dust! Leave it in a conspicuous spot to ensure it is found soon after your love awakens.

Wednesday: Hide one of the quotes you prepared on Monday.

Thursday: Use idea number 23. Wake your mate with your song. If this does not fit your schedule, switch this idea with the quote you have ready for the weekend.

Friday: Give your mate a greatest fan evening, idea number 53. You should start planning this early in the day to give yourself enough time to write your letter.

Weekend: Hide your second quote.

Congratulations on being romantic for an entire month! Hopefully, by now, you and your mate are reaping the benefits of your newfound or rekindled romance. Now is the time to commit yourself to continuing the good habit you have worked to create for an entire month. Transform the mundane. May your life be filled with magical moments!

Appendix

FATHER'S DAY OLYMPICS

Idea 1:

"Tool Time Theme"

Dear Dad,
Congratulations! You have been selected to participate in THE TOOL TIME Father's Day Olympic Games. Tim Allen and Bob Villa have gotten together to create the ultimate challenges. You will be competing against 4 other fathers for the title of "Handy Dad of the Year!" Games begin at noon so don't be late. Thanks for being such an awesome dad! RRRR...RRRR...

Sincerely,
Mom and the kids

Schedule of Events

Tool Time Impression
Sawing and Nail Pounding Speed Contest
Spoon Race (Balancing Nuts and Bolts on a Spoon)
Looooongest Burp
Most Accurate Cast (Hula Hoop and Fishing Pole)
Change Sparkplug in Lawn Mower Speed Contest
Remote Control Car Obstacle Course
Best Hamburger Flip

Prizes: Tools!

Idea 2:

"King for the Day"

Your Majesty,

Today is a celebration of Father's Day. In recognition for all your efforts, patience, dedication, and love, you shall be honored as KING FOR THE DAY. Today you shall only be addressed as "Your Majesty." Your every wish is our command. Today everyone is merely your servant.

At 10 o clock your royal presence is requested to compete with 4 other prestigious kings in a heated tradition of games entitled, "The Father's Day Olympics." Please be prompt and ready to compete. You are a wonderful father and today we say thanks and you're doing a great job!

Love,
Mom and the kids

Events

1. Sawing and Nail Pounding Race
2. Limbo Contest
3. Arm Wrestling Contest
4. Carrot Peeling Race
5. Baby Changing Race
6. Egg on a Spoon Race
7. Golf Putting Contest
8. Obstacle Course

Make the kings wear party crowns. Roll
out some red carpet – fabric.

Idea 3:

"The Wild West Time Warp"

Dear Dad,

Yee-Haw Cowboy! You have been warped to the Wild Wild West! You will be competing with 4 other hellions to see who will be declared the rootin tootinest, badest, wildest, gunslingin dad at the Fatherhood Canyon. So grab your cowboy hat and get ready to rumble. Hee-Haw! See ya yonder...

Love,
Mom and the kids

Events

Target Shooting (Dart guns with coke cans)
Spitting Contest
Galloping Contest (Broom as a horse)
Best Draw
Lasso (Rope child's dinosaur)
Cards
The Robber/Saloon Girl Pickup
Watermelon Eating Contest

Yellow the paper invitation using a tea bag. After it dries burn the edges of the paper so it will look really old. Bury the invitations in the backyard and mark the spot with an X. Give each dad a cowboy hat to wear and a shovel to dig up his time warp invitation.

Idea 4:

"The Super Father Bowl"

Dear Mr. Dad,

Congratulations! You have been selected to compete in the 2004 Super Father Bowl Games. Today's events have been designed especially with you in mind.

Games will commence promptly at noon at the _____ field. You will be competing for the grand prize of the 2004 Super Father Bowl ring and title. So get your uniform and get ready to compete!

Love,
Mom and the kids

Line up of Events

Football toss
Gum Spitting Contest
Putt-Putt Contest
Basketball Contest
Limbo
Obstacle Course

The winner will receive a 2004 lollipop Super Father Bowl ring and honorary football signed by the children. Uniforms consist of old t-shirts made by the children with handprints and footprints and the number of kids on the back.

(Other theme ideas include: Pirate Wars, Knight Wars, Soldier Games, Mission Impossible, Terminator, and Men in Black themes!)

Sample Bank Statement #24:

THE BANK OF LOVE
1 Adoration Lane
Heart City, US XXXOO

<u>Deposits</u>

Took the dog out so I could sleep in	$5,000	
Brought me a cup of tea	$1,000	
Cleaned off my car	$2,000	
Bathed little Johnny	$10,000	
Picked up Lucy from ballet	$2,000	
Left a love note under my pillow	$1,000,000	

<u>Withdrawals</u>

Left the seat on the toilet up		$250
Account Balance	*$$$$$$ Rich in LOVE!!!!*	

117

Be as creative as you dare!

Sample Resume #71
RESUME

Objective: To obtain a position as your muse.

Qualifications:
Fantastic baker of chocolate chip cookies, marvelous kisser, sublime sex goddess, articulate banterer, loving, sweet supportive partner.

Experience:
Several years experience refining methods to please my love. Willing to work long hours with no pay. Dedicated to the job and willing to do whatever it takes to satisfy the demands of being your muse.

Tip:
Hurry and grant me the position so I can begin inspiring you right away!

La Tara

Appetizers

Nachos
Marshmallows

Entrees a la Tara

Steak um sandwich
Dead cow, mayo, bread.

Spaghetti
Special recipe includes sugar.

Desserts

3 Kisses
one playful kiss, one lingering kiss, one sweet kiss a la
Tara.

Hugs
2 big hugs a la Tara.

Sample really bad jokes #14:

Why did the monkey fall out of the tree?
He was dead.

How do you make holy water?
Boil the hell out of it.

Why didn't the skeleton cross the road?
He didn't have the guts.

Quick Quotes

"I love thee with the breath, smiles, tears, of all my life." –*Elizabeth Barrett Browning*

"A happy marriage is a long conversation which always seems too short." –*Andre Maurois*

"To get the full value of joy you must have someone to divide it with." -*Mark Twain*

"Love sought is good, but given unsought is better." – *William Shakespeare*

"Where there is love there is life." –*Gandhi*

"There is only one happiness in life: to love and be loved." –*George Sand*

"Who, being loved, is poor?" –*Oscar Wilde*

"Love cannot be bought except with love." – *John Steinbeck*

The Daily Romantic Checklist

☐ Tell my partner 4 things I am grateful for today.

☐ Do one romantic gesture to show how much I care.

☐ Say I love you.

Reflect on the magical moments you have created and will continue to create.

Index

If you would like to share your ideas or stories on creating relationship magic send them to:

100 Magical Moments
C/O Beatify Books
PO Box 140
Kingmont, WV 26578

Or visit us online at:
100magicalmoments.com